Driftwood

Driftwood

Expressive Poetry from a Mental Health Journey

Martha Craig
Illustrated by Evan Jackson

TABLELAND PRESS

Copyright © 2024 Martha Craig
Driftwood: Expressive Poetry from a Mental Health Journey by Martha Craig
Cover and interior illustrations by Evan Jackson

Copyright © 2011, 2024 Martha Lynn Craig
The following poems: "Alex," "An Artist in Everyday Clothing," "Anointed One," "Broken and Poured Out," "Every Girl," "How Beautiful," "I Walk," "Juicy," "Moments by Martha," "Queen of Hearts," "Quiet I Am," "Sabbath Wisdom," "Stand Still," "Stranger on My Own Path," "Symphony of a Woman," "The Divorce Dragon," and "Wired."

All rights reserved. No portion of this book may be reproduced, stored in a retrieval system, or transmitted in any form or by any means, mechanical, electronic, photocopying, recording, or otherwise, without written permission from the author.

Published in the USA by

TABLELAND PRESS LLC
www.tablelandpress.com
info@tablelandpress.com

ISBN 978-1-949323-13-9 (hardcover)
ISBN 978-1-949323-14-6 (paperback)
ISBN 978-1-949323-15-3 (ebook)

All Scripture quotations are taken from *The Amplified® Bible (AMPC)*, Copyright © 1954, 1958, 1962, 1964, 1965, 1987, by the Lockman Foundation. Used by permission. (www.Lockman.org.) All rights reserved.

Printed in the United States of America.

For Evan

*For all those who feel the stigma and
pain of a mental health journey and
to those who endeavor to help us.*

Bravery is not the absence of fear but perseverance in living through difficulties and believing beyond all measure you have a destiny greater than your circumstances.

—Martha Craig

Contents

Preface	xiii
Acknowledgments	xv

Adorned by Nature

Moonlight	3
Lips to Reply	4
Salvation	5
Standing in the Deep	6
Every Girl	7
Juicy	8
Symphony of a Woman	9

The Reverence

Surrender	13
Beauty Mark	14
Painting in Ball Gowns	15
Piece of Clay	16
Blind	17
Dance	18
Parts of Gray	19
A Distant Land	20
Some Days	21
In the Stillness	22
Anointed One	23
How Beautiful	24
I Walk	25
Sabbath Wisdom	26
Stand Still	27
As the Spirit Leads	28

Naked Soul
By Invitation Only	31
Ordinary Girl	32
The Child Within	34
Expired Meters	35
Driftwood	36
Good Intentions	37
Coloring within the Lines	38
Spinning Circles	39
Beneath My Skin	40
Invisible	41
The Door	42
Bare	43
Finding Myself	44
If Truth Be Told	45
A Bridge	46
The Question	47
Grief	48
An Artist in Everyday Clothing	49
Broken and Poured Out	50
Moments by Martha	51
Queen of Hearts	52
Quiet I Am	53
Stranger on My Own Path	54
The Divorce Dragon	56
Wired	57
Longing for Love	58

Gratitude of the Heart
Miracles by Design	61
Evan	62
A Cord Not Easily Broken	63
The Diva	65
Undeniable Gift	66
Sisters	67
The Voice of Love	68

Moonchild	69
Ann	70
The Sacred Oath	71
We Still Will	72
The Blessing of Ellie Florene	73
Hallowed Ground	74
Relevant Wisdom	76
Light One Candle	77
Love Unimaginable	78
Debbie	79
DJ in Disguise	80
Alex	81
This Setting Place	82
Melting into Arms	83

The Evolution of Loss

Lonely	87
Cry	88
Body of Proof	89
Black and White Frame	90
Stuck	91
Fingers on a Hot Stove	92
Cardboard Box	93
Tightrope	94
Human	95
Remember	96
The Crooked Line	98
Carried like the Wind	99
On My Own Terms	100
The Waiting Game	101
Purple Haze	102
Broken Wings	103
The Cost of Love	104
Abandonment	105
The Burden of Silence	106
Lies	107

Survival Mode	108
Obscurity	109
The Depths of Loneliness	110
Clubs in a World of Diamonds	111
Sadness in the Air	112
Stone Cold	113
Trapped	114
Silence the Madness	115
Bones, Bones, Bones	116
The Forgotten Ones	117
Threading Needles	118
Sorrow Land	119
The White Pillowcase	120
Blank	121

Hope Rising

Lay It Right Down	125
Battleground	126
Mercy	127
New Glasses	128
I Am More	129
Revolution	130
Making Changes	131
Standing Firm	132
Like a Cat with Nine Lives	133
Wounds in All of Us	134
Unfamiliar Places	135
Awakening	136
This Road I've Walked	137
Courage	138
While Looking	139
Fly	140
The Power to Transform	141
Fierce	142
The Bravery of Power	143
Warrior	144

The Struggle	145
The Secret Key	146
The Open Door	147
The Meaning of Love	148
Turn Around	149
Waking Up	150
My Life Rising	151
Morsel of Faith	152
Back from the Abyss	153
Before Midnight	154
The Other Given Half	155
Sunshine	156
Lemons for Breakfast	157
Stronger	158
Remembering Intuitions	159
Called to Live Beauty	160

Preface

This sacred book of poetry invites you to be a part of the company on a soul's journey through my life's quest to find myself in the wanderings of words come to life.

My way has not been an easy one; but if I can help one person, it was worth all the risk. You see, this book is dedicated to all those who sense a loss within themselves. May I and others who know the unrelenting dark places find hope that may be reborn in the bravery of walking through each moment bent on believing in what we cannot conceive. My hope is to share raw honesty through this diary of my life that contains the release of passionate emotions on paper that it might inspire others.

This is hallowed ground—my deepest secrets set to pages. I am transparent in letting you walk where few people have tread that you might begin to understand.

If you or someone you know is struggling with thoughts of harm or is in mental health distress, please contact the Suicide and Crisis Prevention Lifeline by calling or texting 988.

Acknowledgments

While I was writing this book, I began to question how my words would ever reach people in order to make a difference. I am grateful for Margaret, who offered to edit and publish my work after hearing some pieces of my poetry. Without God's graciousness and her extraordinary kindness to help and encourage me throughout this process to publish this work of art, it would not exist. There were days of fear and depression, but Margaret was a light in a sometimes-cloudy storm. I owe her a deep debt of infinite gratitude and love. She is the bond that helped glue this body of work together.

For my beautiful nephew, Evan, who was generous enough to sketch these amazing visual representations for the book. Your childlike spirit is a little piece of heaven I will always treasure. These remarkable illustrations remind me of the talented art created by your hands. You were and always will be fiercely loved and missed every day. Being kind was just your demeanor, and honesty surrounded your smile.

For Matt, my son, you teach me the wonder of an ordinary day and make me want to be the best version of perseverance I hold in my hands. Entering the room, I am grateful for the moments spent together. Love has granted us this time with hearts held in measured language.

This book is also dedicated to my mom and dad. They have shown me grace, faith, love, and a need for being kind. Always seeing the good in others, they have taught me genuine forgiveness. Thank you, Mom and Dad, for always being an incredible support of my poetry. I love you both like the sunshine dries up all the rain.

For Sam, my partner, my love, who taught me to let go of my hurt. An extraordinary man, you bring true joy to me, like the sound of the ocean is to my heart. My love for you is effervescent in a world that needs hope and comfort you impart. You are a shinning beacon like the light that you are. My life is enriched because of your bravery to be such a good man. Thank you for the acceptance of all that I am.

For some years, I have had the privilege to know a gentleman and great friend of mine, Bill. He has supported and motivated my work during the entire process. He is a true friend and confidant in every sense of the meaning. Immeasurable companionship comes forth to meet us as we gather laughter once more. Your constant, abiding love helped me believe in myself when I did not think myself a poet. Thank you for the profound effect you have had on my life.

For my family, thank you for your support during this journey and your motivation to help me to be the best version of myself.

Adorned by Nature

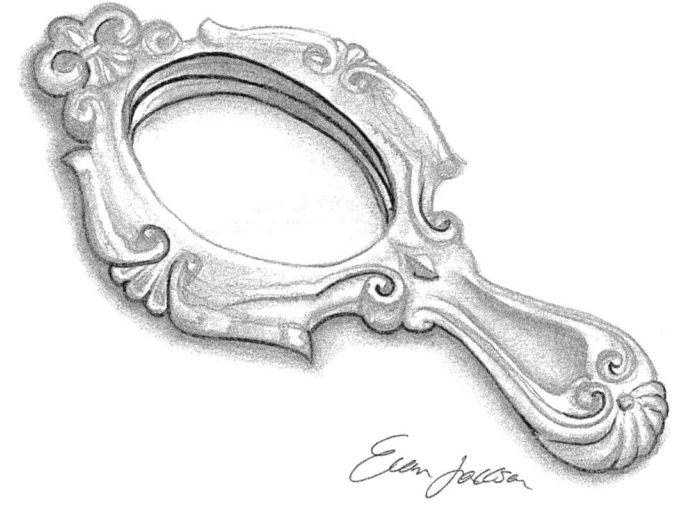

O Lord, our Lord, how excellent (majestic and glorious) is Your name in all the earth! You have set Your glory on [or above] the heavens.

Psalm 8:1

Moonlight

All I can see is
moonlight since
I met you in a
fresh notation
of curls,
headed down a
path of no return,
only to be
held in motivation
by your smile.

Shine, sleepy head.
You leave me
breathless in a
world of music.
Be careful with
my emotions
sought in Memphis,
when wished upon
a shooting star.

I can't breathe
when you are
next in line to
sit beside me,
while the gentleness
of you surprises me,
as your sheer comfort
tells the story
behind the anticipation.

Lips to Reply

Let love dream a little while in
sleepy slumber, just beyond
words that carry heartfelt
sentiments, showing me with
arms and kisses, daring my
lips to reply.

You're the melody my soul is
longing to intertwine, held
captive by your strength. To read
between the lines becomes clear.

Run to me, and I will give all I
have to offer. When the evening
is through, the hour of midnight
comes to a close, and so it warrants
more than a lost shoe.

Salvation

Salvation feels so great when
You look at me with those
beautiful eyes—turned me inside
out. Press me against the glass
with sunshine you share.

Oceans rumor waves of love,
when bare feet run to You in
sands of time. Resting in Your
arms of comfort—give it right back.

My heart fights the right to
believe in hope tonight, when
souls collide with truth in how
we connect through music
in the moonlight.

Standing in the Deep

Love stands to show a part of me;
so deep dive in with both feet,
if you dare.

For I imprint all goodness within
my soul to be counted as one
who does not bring up twisted
lines, but fully proves that I am
trustworthy of the relationship,
which started the symphony.

Relish in each tender moment,
for it passes so quickly. Feel my
heartbeat when you accept
those imperfections, which I
choose to see as an essential
piece of the puzzle.

Patiently waiting for the day
when you land straight in my
arms, holding me tight as if you
believe in giving hope a new name.

Every Girl

Every girl
just wants
to find
within herself
the dance
she knows
belongs to
the heart
she gives
to a
raging world
that covers
her true
identity.

Hope rests
tonight when
she reveals
her humanity
in an
honest interpretation
of the
soul that
creates a
reason to
celebrate the
beauty of
every girl.

Juicy

Life embraces passion
as I open my eyes
to new wanderings.
Drinking in the miracle
of an ordinary day
makes me long to
bask in creative displays
of abandonment.
Playful nudgings move
through unspoken lips,
declaring the natural
desire within.

Symphony of a Woman

Forged in the
essence of
divine beauty,
inspiring the
world to move
between a
symphony higher
than heaven's
breath.

Draws forth
the birth of
love to a
kindred heart
yielding the
portrait of an
everlasting masterpiece
known only
by way of
her exquisite
soul.

The Reverence

*God said, Do not come near; put your
shoes off your feet, for the place on
which you stand is holy ground.*

Exodus 3:5

Surrender

I run to You when all else
fails, for I am lost in Your love.
So come find me like a precious
coin You sought in a corner
once a long time ago.

Arms outstretched catch me.
Embraced in Your net cast over,
grace given freely overwhelms
my mind. How long have You
been waiting?

Wondering what to do in this big
world You've planned. Simply
coming home to the fresh new
start You offer every day, if I open
my eyes to You and pray.

I surrender!

Beauty Mark

I feel Your presence, and it
leaves a beauty mark across
my tortured soul, waiting for
the day to see the brilliance
of Your face.

Crossing deserts is what You
do to seek me, even though
I am distracted and miss Your
unconditional love like forgetting
a divine appointment.

Come find me and mend the
broken places. I so desperately
seek to be resurrected by You,
unfulfilled in this so sedentary
place.

Painting in Ball Gowns

Knock, and I usher in romantic notions
    in my gaze turned upward as I see
You approach gently to heal my scars,
    joyfully resting in Your arms of love,
if I take time to worship.

Painting in ball gowns is what I do best.
    For You have set me free from the bondage
that used to harbor my mind's eye, seeing
    a new face looking back at me.

Piece of Clay

It is in the absolute silence I hear
    You speak to me, calling my name,
and wonder how long You have
    tenderly knocked at the door.

I wait expectantly to hear everyday
    love songs poured out from Your
mouth over me. For I give You
    highest praise my lonely soul
creates out of raw canvas.

You seek after me even when
    I run down a troubled path,
stopped by Your sweet ways
    melting into a simple piece of clay.

Blind

I could not see Your miraculous
    grace before me, for I was
stumbling in the dark, blind to
    Your fire rising up toward Heaven
in my name.

Slowly, I see Your powerful words
    speak healing to eyes that could
not see Your miracle ways reaching.
    The core of limitless possibilities fall
over me when You take my right
    hand and hold it during my darkest
days.

All praise is given to Him who is lifted
    high, for there is none greater to give
blessings bestowed upon. His love is
    everlasting in the day of my salvation.

Dance

Rivers part when I run with
    holy feet, deciding I am worthy
of Your endless love which
    beckons me—peace to still
myself in the eye of raging
    waters surrounding.

Light my life so others may see
    Your glory shown down to comfort
the brokenhearted, returning
    hope restored where once
was broken.

Dance for joy as You sing over
    me with abiding compassion.
Cover all the worries of today.
    Live life with each moment of
shared bliss or you might miss your
    intended blessing.

Parts of Gray

As I seek Your face, I lift up
humble hands, all I have to
offer to such fierce beauty.
Now fall on knees with reverent
heart to reveal Your perfume,
which fills this space, knowing
You were looking for me.

Arms around tight feel so good
to be home. Where have I been
walking all this time down a dark
and stormy night? No more
condemnation; all that perfection
gone. Parts of gray feel fine.

Praise You for You have called me
by a new name to redeem what
was lost. For I am renewed, and
hope soars within my soul when
You dare to give me the desires
of my heart.

A Distant Land
(A Love Poem)

When I let go of all imperfections,
trusting God to show up, learning to
be myself, resting in His presence
surprises even me. That's when
my beauty arrives from a distant land.

Speaking words of comfort, I cover
your wounds, desiring the wisdom to
let you be your true self, fully disclosing
the knowledge of who I am without
pretension or fear, drawing you closer to Me
who has written strength in the palm
of My hand.

Some Days

Unsure, I am shy in my approach,
yet I do not believe sometimes
the truth spoken by You who
restores all my hidden pain.

Some days I just can't fathom
Your costly love, and confusion
is pulled by the weight of shoulders
piled high.

That's when You rescue me from
my own insecurities with unending
songs of grace, as I sit and ponder
tender romantic words I long to
hear—soothing each sorrow—casts
out all fear.

In the Stillness

In the stillness of heaven's
breath, I see Your beauty
crying out for divine words
to express inexplicable joy.
You call to me.

Only love stood firm forever
kept, for I was searching a new
way set wielding a course;
mark my life.

Anointed One
(Based on Psalm 61)

New oil touches my lips.
I taste only gladness
where sorrow once stood.
Your hands give presence
to holy comfort I feel.
Binding my brokenness,
You pray for my double portion.
I receive fresh water
and thirst no more.

How Beautiful

(Jessica, I will never forget how God's
Spirit moved me while I heard you sing
and play your harp so beautifully.)

I heard Your words for the first time in Hebrew, and
tears ran down my cheeks with love, the only
response my heart could reply to the voice that
calls my name written on Your right palm.

How beautiful my Abba, Father, You look tonight,
for I gaze upon Your miraculous goodness and
awe, knowing with a grateful heart I was bestowed a
precious gift of utter grace and mercy to behold
such a sound that only angels must attend.

It is with reverence I usher in Your deepest presence,
having the pleasure of You pierce my weary soul
to soothe it with a miracle in an unlikely and
ordinary place.

Completely transformed, I will never be the same
person I once was for You have opened my eyes
to this new divide I must cross, listening to Your inspired
words set to music so divine.

Waking with my Lover, You are my prized possession.
Daily I see Your sheer glory and can't help but offer
my highest praise to the One whose living power
works through me.

I Walk

(Based on 1 Kings 17:7-16)

Life in order
of randomness,
I walk
as new steps
appear to hover
by faith held
closer, this time
spent trying
to hear
that quiet voice
sent to
whisper answers
of dried brooks
and foreign lands
in hope
to know
I AM.

Sabbath Wisdom

Time,
a little slower
than usual cadence,
brief interlude
of silence
to ponder the
natural progression
of the day's
quiet conversation
with a God who
seeks my attention
to commune with
higher ways.

Sacred day
comes with anticipation
of learning
to make
authentic choices,
creating
moments of grace
in caring for the soul.

Stand Still

My shoes felt
inescapably inadequate
in your presence, Lord.
Those long-abandoned
holy words shouted
in poems to me
directly from
Your glorious mouth.

Breathtaking in awe,
You received me
as I could
see your beauty
radiant and
set to fire.
Angels danced
in sheer glory
causing you to
turn Your head.

Pure love rained
down across my skin,
for thirst is all I know.
There will be
no holding me
back this time.
For I will
stand still and
just let go.

As the Spirit Leads

A better prayerful life offers insight
into convictions felt with deepest
love for You.

Kept promise to God, always having
honest communication—difficult
subjects arise.

Listening to my own advice takes
my breath away as my life seeks
change, as well as taking to heart
as the Spirit leads.

Naked Soul

*Behold, You desire truth in the
inner being; make me therefore
to know wisdom in my inmost heart.*

Psalm 51:6

By Invitation Only

My voice finally arrived by
invitation only contrived
by a major revolution set
to a tune of life's bliss—
the first mosaic place I
observed this miraculous
explosion of truth.

Now time stands packaged
in virtuous echoes believing
the incandescent syllables
spoken were captured by
a momentary pause
given to enchantment.

Ordinary Girl

I am just an ordinary girl
who bleeds when she is
cut by life's nasty
hateful cries telling her
she is different from
all the rest. Does it
ever really end?

Life hurts when you
cannot seem to find
someone with arms
to share the pain inside
that wraps around your
aching soul. Twisted lies
imitate the truth, running
down this path of no
return. Somehow, I cannot
see the sun.

Silence is my cover friend,
betraying who I really am.
Only God knows my true soul.
No one else took the time
to ever really know what
hides behind the mask I bear.

Now that I have borne it well
with life so desolate and full
of despair, in need of comfort
and of grace from human hearts
so kindred dear. Hear me in my
hour so bleak that I am just
an ordinary girl!

The Child Within

The starting line always looks daunting
    as I press my nose to the unforgiving
glass, yet my unwavering faith is
    stronger.

Give me a chance to show up ready
    to win this fight for the never-ending
battle of will versus concave reality—
    better known as life.

Early I rise to prepare each day,
    dancing to my own lyrical music
heard inside, ready to partake in
    healing the child within.

Expired Meters

In the end, does it really matter
that this world ever listens to my
story? No one seems to care, so
self-absorbed with themselves
in a pattern of loud noises clanging
around me like a piece of corn
stuck in my throat.

People carry on with busy lives
next to grand central parking in
uneven lines with expired meters,
not even looking up to give a
surprise greeting to a stranger now
and again, tailgating through life
as if the next social media gadget
is more important that the neighbor
they never knew.

Driftwood

Let me come down for I am
a princess in a tower of my
mind, withering away in this
place of absolution, turning
a blind eye to what I have
become.

Beauty in its essence has
gone and faded from my
eyes. How long must I be a
cautionary tale to those
around me?

Weary, I yearn to see what
lies behind these outside
walls of countless hours,
hoping there is more to
me than endless driftwood.

Good Intentions

I am cursed to roam this world
with good intentions that go to
some unknown force beckoning
to be pulled in another direction
that is some innate chemical
reaction in my brain, taking over
like a prison storm.

Tip the balance scales, and I
become someone I do not
recognize at times, making
infinitely different choices.
Drawn as a moth to a flame, I
can't look back, holding on course
in a path I know I'll regret.

Coloring within the Lines

Run away my heart, for I stay afraid to let you
be vulnerable to paint the canvas of who I
really am, seeking solace in this weary world
of cold isolation, always watching from
inside the gate.

Too cruel this world has been of late
for me to venture a new starting block.
Always coloring within the lines, I walk
as not to offend, never daring to open this
mystery called life.

Spinning Circles

I could be in a room full of people
and still feel like the loneliest,
most invisible person facing the
endless voices that refuse to halt.

Somehow, I escape to my little
observation corner and see perfect
people, unlike me (out of place where
no one bothers to really get to know
the girl who feels different from all
the rest). Spinning circles inside my head
make me nauseous and overwhelm the mind.

Deepest love is all I have left to offer
if someone could take the time to
unearth it. But until this miracle happens,
I am doomed to walk this world in great
solitude unimaginable.

Beneath My Skin

I am like an onion with many
different layers that few peel
because they are afraid to see
what lies beneath my skin.

Fear comes to mind, gripping
those who don't want to
know the truth behind this
intelligent, sophisticated,
and loving individual, knowing
there is more than meets
the unequivocal eye.

If they only took the time
to but reach inside the
depths of their hearts to
discover a new way of
thinking, they would behold
the way inside this
beautiful prism called me.

Invisible

I feel invisible in this strange
    place we call a world, lost in the
conundrum of life with families
    coming and taking their leave,
shopping for Christmas presents
    they will soon forget were once owned.

I pause to speak, but not even
    the sparrow stops to listen.
Gathered round are those silent
    as the grave, for they haunt
the night passages like an homage
    to the weary loneliness I must endure.

The Door

I dream of a life where I am
heard so easily that truth drops
from lips like ice cream melting
in the summer heat.

Love finds a new way home in
my battered heart to expand reason for
strings pulled tight, so light the way
to help me open the door.

My faith shows how to live in hope
even when gray skies cast a
shadow in the valley of my mind.

My deepest thoughts come to life set me
free into another world, comfortable in my
own skin, changing my life with each word
I recite.

Bare

Bare of all my makeup, I feel
naked and exposed to the girl
I am afraid everyone can see, the
imperfections in daylight, hidden
behind the mask.

People say I am pretty, but
somehow, I cannot fathom the
compliment in my convoluted
mind, seeing the opposite of
what the mirror reveals.

Finding Myself

Realizing I have power and accepting
truth is the best place for finding myself
within this menagerie.

Seeing my reflection beyond the broken
slit of a mirror leads me down an open
path of kindness, shows up to greet the
other side of daylight—right between
the eyes of beauty to stay.

New, reborn, riding on the wings of Venus
herself, I learn with every heartache, choosing
lessons of survival instead of pity, staying
close to wisdom's door.

If Truth Be Told

If truth be told, I could never
measure expectations embedded
before me, for I hear them ever
listening to my mind's conversation.

Take me down off these platform
shoes, so high it's getting cold and
lonely on this never-ending circus
ride.

The pressure, so relentless, breaks
my childlike heart—seeing my
imperfections but unsure how to
move beyond this vicious cycle
once more.

A Bridge

There is a bridge I see
in my mind's eye if only
to cross with wisdom
intact. Fluidly it appears,
if only for a moment's
glance.

I want to transport
to cities unknown.
Beckoning me, they
call as if to say I was
born to taste chance.

The Question

Is there some written law that
precludes everyone to ask you
what you do for a living?

I maintain there is more to me.
Sing a new verse.

What if we were to skip that
question? Would we know
ourselves or be lost without
an answer—a puzzle with
missing pieces?

Grief

The pain surrounds me
wrapped like a curtain
that chokes with every
swallow I take when the
night comes calling my name.

I miss you like my heart
stops beating against the
headboard, lying there
succumbing to the heaviness
of my dreams.

An Artist in Everyday Clothing

Changing, and no power
is able to stop me.
This transformation happens
as if God has opened me
and will not allow anyone
to shut the box.
I am drawn as a moth
to the light, and
I can't get enough of it.

Not satisfied with
where I am, but
don't know where to be.
Wanting to free fall as
a new spirit into
some undreamt possibility.

Finally alive, just
waking up from a
thousand deaths.
Colors swirl all
around and dance
in my mind—
an artist in
everyday clothing.

Broken and Poured Out

Tiny shards,
   pieces
surrender—
   falling, falling.

Once a vessel,
   a recognizable tool,
no longer distinguished between
   original design or new creation.

Pain of rebirth,
   violent affliction,
poured out and offered,
   emptied,
only to be filled by You.

Moments by Martha

Wrapped in a curtain
of long-standing
proper words expressed
in kitchen soap
up to my elbows,
hiding behind the
scenes, a canvas
yet to be painted.

Tasks given, not
wanted by others
without sought
opinion or foreground.
Walking in limelight,
seeking this
passionate life I
have cause to
endeavor.

Carry my heart
gently as I was
always meant to
sing the way home.
For comfort lies
in the relaxed fit
of my own skin
shamelessly showing
no fear.

Queen of Hearts

No flowers,
my own chocolate,
dressed in pink.
Heavy-hearted,
alone—
I think
this time
it will be
my turn
to see that
right now
it's okay
to just be
with me.

Quiet I Am

Quiet I am
   and solitary inside.
I am slowly dying
   from a shattered life,
torn glass shards
   ever glued to my
heart seeing the
   world through
a kaleidoscope
   of mistrust.
I stand in a
   minefield of indecision,
based on a life
   of confinement
and perfection
   to be someone else,
never given the
   strength to find
the voice inside
   crying,
so desperately wanting
   to be.

Stranger on My Own Path

Deep in a dark
theater of loneliness,
I bury my thoughts
low in misery
to tell a story,
which consists of
being by myself
for a greater portion
of the agenda.

It is all consuming
to be alone
without another
person for any
kind of sweet-
comfort touch
or be loved by
a soul mate.

So, I must remain
in limbo. For now
is not the time to
connect with the
universe's way
of separation, which
on some level never
ceases to leave me
feeling like a
stranger on my
own path, walking
around in my
underwear.

The Divorce Dragon

How can one day
   turn significant dreams
into streams of horror
   that scream fury
and poise for
   no end in sight?

Right before my eyes,
   this day changed to
black and simple-edged
   circus mirrors,
scarred for life.

No room within
   my mind for
evil comments made
   in jest to break
my heart on barriers
   too many to count
or hurdle by way
   of treading water.

Let me refrain
   from this utterly
wrenching display
   of cookie-cutter
souls sliced ripe
   to mimic a
solitary ballet.

Wired

Walking around in a circle,
this anxiety-driven rampage
needs some room to breathe
before its neon head raises
in disdain to chase fallen
dreams far from spotlight.

Unforgiven moments of fear
cross my mind and race toward
bearings that seek to serve
only those that follow
a cavern of unknown proportions,
surrendering a hurricane
of insanity once inside.

Longing for Love

I've become a backdrop to some
    kind of one-sided popsicle that
falls in your lap when you least
    expect it, leaving a stain that
refuses to be removed.

Loving someone who does not
    love you back hurts like a fog
you can't see through—trapped,
    running for the antidote.

Gratitude of the Heart

Every good gift and every perfect (free, large, full) gift is from above; it comes down from the Father of all [that gives] light, in [the shining of] Whom there can be no variation [rising or setting] or shadow cast by His turning [as in an eclipse].

James 1:17

Miracles by Design

(For my son, Matt, whom I raised every day in
my heart as I walked in a covenant with God,
knowing you will always be forever loved by the
woman who was truly faithful.)

Pieces missing in my heart
render the longing of
seeing your face
reflected in part.

Seeking God's will and
sealing our fate
by love and strength
that was dictated
by certainty for your
best interest to open
a door, yet
shutting the gate.

Hearing your voice
for the very first time,
and humbled with
who you are,
lets me know
it was really
God's miraculous design.

Evan

(With love, from your aunt)

Living the dream through
    my eyes, open images of
things to come, bear witness
    to the oracle of art
given in return for talent
    rendered.

Why not bring down the
    shattered screen to remake
the sun? Transfer life to those
    spoken in name only.

Strong I stand to see this
    new creation envelop over
me, as I am thirsty for new
    adventure to behold.

With ink in my right hand,
    I turn ideas into well-thought
plans with great precision, for
    I was born to be a gifted man.

A Cord Not Easily Broken

(For Bill, my dearest friend, who accepts me for
who I am and never fails to believe in me)

A cord not easily broken
binds my transparent soul
to a man who sees the
depths of me. Sing me comfort
in the night for you reach
where the silent tears fall.

Honest words speak
volumes to my heart
when your presence
fills the room. Come to
my side for I vow my friendship,
surrendering my life
in your hands.

Care I not if the moon
looks upon the stars with
such brilliance until You
see my face shining up
at Yours? Longing to be
held, placed only in the
embrace of the One whose
kindred spirit intertwines.

With honesty written on Your right palm,
I set my name across the
fire that burns for You.
Blessings deep come down
when fixed in the exquisite
gallery of sanctuary.

The Diva

She sits behind the spotlight, ready
to take the stage, dressed to kill. No
mortal ever knew such beauty came forth
from red lips poised in silhouette.

There is sadness in her eyes most
people miss, but she will never let them
in to see the hurt she must hide, revealing
true lies behind the smoke of black and
white cigarettes.

The bright lights came, and she answered
the call to stand through the screams
in stilettos, for she's known both heaven
and hell, a fighter, who in the end, calls
pride her closest friend.

Undeniable Gift

(For my brother, David, who always
makes me laugh. With love.)

Forward thinker beyond our present
    time, lending moral presence to
those in need of courage and strength
    who lean on arms covered with
stories of encouragement.

Your independent wit and
    wisdom are an undeniable
gift for those who are privileged
    to know you.

With a free spirit, may you
    boldly reach for dreams unseen
when you believe in miracles
    with childlike faith, being
true to yourself.

Sisters

I really don't know at which
point the courses merged,
like a hurricane running
down a stream riding high.

Seeing is believing, and I
still remember you as a
little girl, as gentler times float by.

Holding hands before bedtime
at Grandma's house loaned
comfort to a sisterly
bond I will never forget.

Running towards you, I take hold
the vine that forever binds us
to a love surrounded by time.

The Voice of Love

(For my mother and father, on their
fiftieth wedding anniversary.
All my love.)

"Forever, and the rest is history,"
sang the little chapel on the hill,
when he asked, and she said yes
to the greatest love story this
family has ever known.

Only the heart can tell time that
it has been but a moment in
passing glances, as the two of you
read between the lines when
promises have lasted for a lifetime.

In this fiftieth-year anniversary,
let your timeless love and
boundless grace lead you through
life, holding onto memories so
dear and precious times to come,
guiding your way. Always rejoice in
the moment, as those who surround
you are here to celebrate by your side.

Moonchild
(For Chandra)

Moonchild, I am, set to light in
    playful wanderings when the
wind blows through my mind
    as I remain a strong woman
within the collage.

In solitude I find myself in black
    and white sequences, resurrecting
hope once banished from detail,
    fixated on artful living.

Helping others is my gift in need,
    soothing the jagged edge that
so desperately needs healing within
    each sacred place, grateful for humor
bestowed to ease the suffering.

Ann
(A tribute, with love)

Your light dispersed, exchanged for
angelic wanderings we don't always
understand.

You are grace in picturesque form,
standing there at the throne next to
God with your name called in deepest
affection; although here on earth, your
faithfulness and moments of great joy
poured out will be remembered forever
as your calling.

I hear peace resounding to those you
love most, saying this is but a journey, and
your wisdom imparted remains within us.
So let heaven rejoice to receive one such
soul whom we were blessed to have walked
among our lives.

The Sacred Oath

(For Dr. Khan, who helped me in
the dark places to see the light)

Wisdom and great knowledge imparted
without judgment have led me on this
journey of much needed strength and care.

Loving myself, as I do so freely with others,
can only be taught by the bravest of hearts.
Believing in the encouragement found in your
words binds up wounds.

Insightful, you know when the woman or the
child is ever present, speaking from the sacred
oath, always gentle with my spirit, trusting each
other with respect.

We Still Will

(A tribute for my dad,
who meant the world to me.)

We still will go for drives together
    in the sunshine with the windows
rolled down, while we swap
    stories and you chauffeur me
around like James Bond.

We still will stop for ice cream
    cones or coffee when we
feel like it, yours with the cone
    up, mine down, and one for
Mom.

You still will give me good
    advice when I need it, pray
for me, or see how the laughter
    comes easily in the midst of
it all.

We still will watch great movies
    in the sunroom and eat buttered
popcorn to our delight.

We still will hold hands in the
    knowledge that this dance
called love lasts forever.

The Blessing of Ellie Florene

One pink bow turns a head,
for happiness overflows like a
newfound spring of water.

Beauty and grace follow your footsteps.
Grow like a weed catching
a butterfly's cocoon.

Sing a sweet lullaby of
forget-me-nots over your pillow,
rejoicing in the vision God has planned.

Hallowed Ground

(To Will and Opal. Written after
standing on my grandparents' graves.)

Sacred place reserved
for resting souls
of purposeful living.

I set my feet
on hallowed ground
of those who came
before me, and
felt the wind rush
swirling around my
mind of lessons learned
and imprints of memories
embedded in my soul.

Pieces of me
scattered abound as
we are woven together
for that moment,
leaving only a
marker for disguise,
knowing that I will
remember seeing your
face in the grand,
tall trees that
surrounded the common
ground we shared.

Ask, and I shall remove
my shoes, deep
in the presence
of holy territory,
if only to
cry at the mention
of your name.

Relevant Wisdom

Straight into my heart, you
    arrived on the scene as if an
angel split the heavens.

Finding your own path
    seems convoluted, torn
between two worlds, not
    sure where you belong.

Monumental are love's
    choices we make in this
life when presented with
    the most relevant wisdom.

Light One Candle

Light one candle in the darkness,
for your love surrounds and
keeps us remembering the sweet
memories we shared.

Burn it bright, for your presence
is always with us like a warm fire
on a snowy day.

Let us give thanks for the time
we had together and the peace
that is found if we just
light one candle.

Love Unimaginable
(For Sam, my forever love)

You taught me to be strong
beyond belief. See with one
eye; hear with one ear. Hard
as iron reminds me of today's
talk, unimaginable.

Friends on new territory, feeling
our way forward, ironing out
changes on the horizon.

Stars collide with the love I
will always have for you until
death takes my hand. No man
may steal or borrow this time
from me.

Say anything but goodbye, and break
my heart forever. Run to the
other side of the ocean, and
remember to call my name in the
middle of the night.

Debbie

(For my sister. May these kind words convey a
mere part of the deep love I have for you.)

See how the hat fits so beautifully,
calling laughter in your voice
I heard spoken as a daydream.

Singing comes natural like daisies
in springtime, woven in creative
spirit; musicals bend your heart.

Touch the moon, and miracles
show in time, for breath crumbles
surrounded by whispered notes
on a page—set the world on fire.

DJ in Disguise
(For Bill)

Music has been ingrained in your heart, beating in time to a celestial place. It transports to a simpler time.

Listening, I hear many stories told about musicians and songs—a DJ in disguise.

Love to hear the words in your voice, calling to remember when knowledge imparted is sacred.

Looking in your eyes, I see a bond we will forever share. Sing over me with elation, as a reminder of who you are.

Alex
(For the cat next door)

Butterscotch and white
lies down to drink
of the elixir of the
elusive socked foot,
weaving in and out
of affectionate embrace,
only to be held captive
by the late summer sun.

This Setting Place

The day you died, the sun cried
to the moon, "I will become
this setting place."

Press not the flowers to bloom,
for even the soil gives birth to
sorrow; bent trees lie low.

Grief like a storm overhead that
overwhelms the soul until
healing delivers some semblance
of spring.

Melting into Arms
(For Sam, who shares my heart)

Jump into the perfect storm.
Hold my heart beating like
drums poised high.

Overflow continues until joy
bursts forth into the flowers
of my soul. Seeing your face,
I believe in the oracle of a
beautiful day.

Bring your thoughts around
my curly head drowned in
feelings of honest desire.
Moonlight is the taste on your
lips, counting time until I see
you again.

Turning the pages of time, it's
no wonder I set my way towards
you, needing a sweet taste of
sunshine—melting into arms.

The Evolution of Loss

You number and record my wanderings; put my tears into Your bottle—are they not in Your book?

Psalm 56:8

Lonely

I run out of lines
to say when I am
the only one thinking
about never getting
any return, heartbroken
from the end of the portrait.

Where were you standing
to fight for me until the end of time,
left somewhere in a daze,
lost, cold, and hungry for your
love that was so noble,
every once in a while when
you showed your true colors?

Remember me, for I was
the one you professed to
burn with desire, scarred with
memories held in doubt,
engraved on my soul, marking
the easiest way out.

Cry

Cry for me. I am broken. Spread
my lonely heart to bear for the
totalities of my sacrifice have
come full circle and look for rest
in no place of comfort do I see.

The weight born is impossible to
comprehend for those who think
they know. I am overwhelmed with
unrelenting, crushing bricks walled
with pain like jagged needles closing in.

In desperation, I come to ask for help,
for a God to save my soul that wanders
the planet with infinite wisdom, to
realize that only the forgiven truth can
set me free.

Body of Proof

I lie in a cavern of depression so
deep it overwhelms me whole
for I cannot see the sun. Turn
my head to the right, and yet, I
sense my foot slips as I try to reach
the edge of recognition.

Today seems to lack the necessary
probability of hope set to motion.
Rancid comes the body of proof
to the mind's eye, written in stone
with notions pictured as if realistic
night wanderings come true.

Help me to realize if I hold my
breath under water, my mind
ceases to scream any possible
solution in an airtight vacuum
world. Swimming in a sea of
indecision, I run back and forth
against the numbness I feel. All
I can do is press forward toward
the surface and believe peace
will follow once more.

Black and White Frame

Treat me as if I were a real
person and not some insane
figment of imagination conjured
by your black and white frame.

Share the love you so genuinely
have for others but seem to
scream so easily at me in fits of
self-righteous rage.

I long for you to see me as a
human being, and to hear your
approval just once beckons
me from beyond my measure
of tortured ground.

Stuck

You're going to miss my arms stuck
like candy to a wrapper—so sweet
and smooth to the touch—a price
too high to pay when you left me
on the cold, bare threshing floor.

Where do I go from here, raising
love from the once-stolen miracles
I have come to know centered in
my heart, trying to remember how
it felt the first time you called my name?

Give grace the spotlight to carry me
through the hard rain, struggling as
the night wind whispers rest, and I find
silent wanderings speak peace to my
soul once again.

Fingers on a Hot Stove

"Do you hear my lonely cries?" said
the wolf, for he knew my name
in the river running wild, screaming
for some kind of acknowledgment
that you care.

Mistaken identity—here it goes again.
I thought I saw in mind's eye to trust
another with secrets too soon. Burnt,
so weary of the risk it assumes.

Can't help sharing my power with
the one who holds back, yet I give
all that I am forever, hoping someday
to get the same semblance in return.

Cardboard Box

Mistrust is what I feel locked inside
this cardboard box of your unassuming
ways when they only seem to use
me at the end of the phrase.

Why go on pretending you love me on
a planetary level to hurt my heart, as it
has been done a thousand times remised?

Fly away and leave me in solitary space
once more, lonely, torn, between heaven
and hell, mourning the vanity of my youth
as a counterpoint ever feeling, if for a
moment, words so deeply submerged my
soul refuses to respond.

Tightrope

Placed in a small cell all by myself
on terms that leave me reeling
on a tightrope falling from the
sky, left scarred by your love, never
to find someone else to dance
the fairytale with.

Tears fall down like puddles
when no one looks. For it hurts
to be alone through life when you
see so many happy parades go by.
It's hard to take refuge in solitary
confinement with only misery
as company.

Human

Torment my heart and let it lie dying, since
it was said of all people you understood
and loved me the most.

Are you also able to leave me brokenhearted
like all the others before—abandoned and
alone with only my deepest thoughts for
misery and harsh company?

You knew the incomprehensible story lines
when reading into the pages of my soul,
yet disavowed them on every level, treating
me sometimes like a possession, instead
of an equal.

Human, I will forever be—this high price I
must now pay with frailty as I am often
reminded how the subject of repercussions
flood my very essence, and to this cruel world,
I am lost forever, longing to pick up the pieces
that seem to slip easily through my hands.

Remember

(This piece of poetry was written in the deepest depths of loneliness in the suicidal world of bipolar depression. It is not meant to bring anyone pain but understanding. It may be difficult for some people to read, but I'm just letting you into my heart.)

(If you or someone you love can relate to this poetry or are having these feelings, please reach out to someone or the National Suicide Prevention Lifeline: call or text 988.)

I can remember a beautiful lady
in an unusually stunning purple suit
with gold buttons. She had that "look"
in her eye as she went about her zeal
for life. That woman was me.

Those stolen memories are all that I
have left to remind me of my potential
in the business world as a new college
graduate in the early 1990s.

Many, many years have passed until
now I only conjure my dreams for
they are all I have to cling to. They
are more interesting than my real
life in purple pajamas.

I am a mere semblance of yesterday—
a person I do not want to know
or care to. I have no recognition of
who I am, so why would I want to
live with her anymore.

Really, I'd just rather remember.

The Crooked Line

The water bottle doesn't look
    straight in the crooked line of
my imagination. Creeping thoughts
    of vulnerability seep between
the background of the
    sharp-edged painting.

Help me let go of the control
    I hold so tightly to my closed
voice so I can live again in the
    free lane I call this beautiful life.

Serving is my reward for connecting
    to the world instead of caustic
isolation, bound for promise to
    reach and not judge.

Carried like the Wind

"I am carried like the wind vicariously,"
    said the unforgiving night, climbing
on a high only a love affair with my
    mania can suffice.

Fighting off loneliness is like a drug I
    turn to over and over, wishing to
create change but knowing the
    illusive cure.

Continuing to lose myself and hurt
    others I love is not the driftless path
I want to repeat, and yet, I feel it
    cycling as if pulled by some magnetic
force set to motion.

Cease this madness, and let me get
    off the merry-go-round in a lifetime of
poor decisions keeping me from
    helping to find a healthy way of
displaying my honest heart to the One
    who truly knows me.

On My Own Terms

An elastic band on the verge of
    breaking, my nerves are frayed
by the pushing and pulling of an
    anxiety-driven mind by people
who don't think for a second that
    I might be struggling with issues
far too great.

Tear my soul into tiny pieces never
    to recover from the selfishness
put before me, unless given a
    chance to catch a breath and
resurrect out of darkness once
    more—on my own terms—offering
gentleness to a heart that feels
    forever lost.

The Waiting Game

This heart of mine is scarred, being
broken so many times by others
who take full advantage of the mark
of kindness and goodness I have to
bare, always playing the waiting game.

Continue to pray for the day when all
the pain will go away, left by those
who just wanted to hang around for
the moment, no eyes on the prize,
flattered by all the attention, but
desperately wanting more than is
offered.

Why can't I have the love that flows
so freely by some who reach for
limitless possibilities, while I lie
suffering in silence of agony—cry
myself to sleep—by the wayside of
deep abiding convictions that leave
me breathless, boundaries to spare?

Purple Haze

Everyone walks around me, and
    all I remember is purple haze
surrounding my mind, covering
    the answers I seek within the
weariness of my suppressed
    emotions.

I don't want to feel the full
    totality of loneliness waiting
for its prey so easily, as it has
    so many times, reeling me into
the dungeon of depression.

Imploding on the inside is what
    I am trying to avoid, but I slide
further into this black hole of
    nothingness, ceasing to be the
woman I once recognized.

Broken Wings

How many goodbyes will be
    said and cold-hearted endings
do I have to endure in my
    heavy heart before branches
break this spirit of mine, torture
    me lie dying soul of souls?

Rivers of tears run down endlessly.
    When will I stop to think of how
you abandoned the creed of
    love spoken over me in secret,
supposedly until the end of time?

Broken wings never fly home
    in the dark, for there is no one
to show me the way, other than
    the cold north wind, since the
sun refuses to shine.

The Cost of Love

I miss you, and my heart stops
beating in circadian rhythm
for fear of the pain it might feel
upon return.

Cover with kindness, for I have
often been weary of those who
unintentionally leave behind a
mark I cannot bear to escape,
sensing unfulfilled words taken
lightly by those who swore sacred
possibilities.

Abandonment

The ever-present feeling that gnaws its
pretentious head at my doorstep each
time I am reminded that there is no easy
exit when I feel left alone, to succumb to
my own greatest fear.

Inside, I am scared like a ball of yarn
all rolled up into a pile of mess, trying
desperately to control utter chaos, failing
miserably, holding tighter still, until I learn
to open my hand and let go.

The Burden of Silence

Sitting all alone in the burden
of silence, I hear only the clock
tick for reassurance that the day
will say its goodbyes.

How long must I endure grief and
its nature to prolong the inevitable
bouts of tears and anger that occur
when I least expect the rearing head,
like an unattended movie playing
with no end.

Brokenhearted, I walk weary through
this world, watching others pass by in
slow motion, waiting for normalcy to
rebound into this so-called life. Paint
me a picture in the stillness, trying to
gain strength to command the presence
to resurrect my soul.

Lies

I believed in you, and the lies
you told took a toll down a
one-way road called my heart,
fully offered, with love to spare.
Protection, in retrospect, did not
stand to fight, keeping me from
harms your promises professed.

Do not stare at the sun
for I cannot feel its warmth wrapped
around my lonely arms. Bereft,
feeling only pain inside this body,
begging to escape somehow, inside
terror flows, checking off the list of
abandonment once more.

Reeling from the reality of the
situation, I find myself questioning the
very role of my existence. Waves of
grief swallow me as if to say life will
never move forward.

Survival Mode

Glazed over window,
    inside foggy mind,
seeing through broken glass,
    finding myself in no condition
to concentrate on surroundings.

Lying down is the only pleasure
    I seek, withdrawn, isolated,
between the outside world
    reeling from exhaustion that
haunts.

Survival mode in central
    standard, locked inside walls
that gravitate toward new
    friends, resurrecting a path
needing to be altered.

Obscurity

I am tired of tears suddenly
appearing down my cheeks
like a fountain—no tossing
coins for good luck.

If you ask me why I am
so troubled this moment,
it is easily the reason I ponder a mystery
with no clue, feeling impending obscurity.

Trying to break free of this
ominous cloud surrounding me
envelops my mind,
like a piece of lint stuck to my clothing.

This cycle of loneliness is a curse
in life that hurts like a dagger to the heart,
inserted and twisted when
you least expect it.

The Depths of Loneliness

I have chosen to build steel walls
    to protect at all costs
the depths of me riddled with loneliness—
    cry myself to sleep;
only my soul hears the silence.

This masquerade lasts for a lifetime,
    not easily broken, pieces missing,
never to complete the puzzle.

The shelf stood empty—
    no trophies or accolades for me—
just like a scratched record
    that skips beats of music behind,
leaving you wondering what is absent.

Clubs in a World of Diamonds

Tears pierce like doves crying
when I see the darker side
of me I have grown
to detest.

Trying so hard to spread light,
but all that seems to forfeit
is clubs in a world of diamonds—
not proud of myself or my
readily available actions.

Coming down is never easy,
having to face harsh reality
in this lonely fortress of
pain I have created, always
repeating this curse.

When will I gain some semblance
of my true self, believing
I am underneath all the madness?

Sadness in the Air

There is a sadness in the
air that surrounds every
breath I take. Care not
to let my cautious tears
fall down my blue shirt.

Today, I cannot shake
difficult memories that haunt
my mind, searching for
any semblance of explanations
why.

Stone Cold

When did callous become the norm in your
    world of ignorance gone blind to seek the
truth instead of your own agenda?

You treat me like a doormat of your choosing
    to believe you understand my bipolar, when,
in reality, mistaken identity, here it goes again.

You have distanced yourself from me for
    years, so pretending to know me is like
trying to cage the wind.

My conscience is clear in this regard.
    Anger does not darken my door as
it does your heart grown stone cold.

Trapped

Tears creep down my face at
the reality between us, caught
in a web of truth for fear of what
may come to light.

Many years have gone by, only
to see selfishness take control
like a thunderstorm rolling over
a mighty sea.

Silence the Madness

Silence the madness inside my head
    ruminating over and over the guilt,
like a cocktail drunk the night
    before, leaving your head spinning.

Spending money is my drug of
    choice, which causes terms of
surrender to the tears which
    so easily fall down my face.

My life lies in ruins, for caustic
    pleasures took control and
would not let go of all I hold dear.

Bones, Bones, Bones

Changing my life forever,
like needles set in stone,
grinding their way into
my bones.

Bones, bones, bones,
turning inward, deteriorating
when they should be summoned
and placed.

Placed with foreign objects
in hopes that pain rejects my
body, asking to darken the door.

The Forgotten Ones

Population explosion to an homage
to those of us who have lived the
hurt side of time with tears running
down imaginary cheeks.

Faces see only what they want to
hear. The night screams can't shake
the abyss that haunts.

Hard stories are for sharing, not for
covering up the grave. Sand just gets
in your mouth; it is time to speak your truth.

Gentleness in listening gives birth
to help heal the scar that ripped open
the soul.

Threading Needles

My head sees with two eyes that
    conjure more than one explosive
reckoning. There is a continual
    argument that scratches like
nails on a chalkboard.

Threading needles of pain never
    seem to end. The storyline
continues to converse upside
    down—letters seemingly
disappear.

Sorrow Land

It's not a surprise to see
my name in lights, crashing
cymbals in my ears full
of cotton, bleeding to be
heard.

Fatigue lines the shelves of
the heart's mass casualty
in Sorrow Land.

The White Pillowcase

Can't lift my head off the
    white pillowcase these so
infamous days. Anxiety
    takes a forefront on the
topic of the latest news
    broadcast in my mind.

Misery is my comfort
    friend, sifting through
this cloud of nothingness
    that succumbs my very
existence.

Blank

The pain surrounds me, wrapped
like a curtain that chokes with
every swallow I take, when night
comes calling my name.

I miss you like my heart stops
beating against the headboard,
lying there succumbing to the
heaviness of my dreams.

Hope Rising

*I have strength for all things in Christ
Who empowers me [I am ready for anything
and equal to anything through Him
Who infuses inner strength into me;
I am self-sufficient in Christ's sufficiency].*

Philippians 4:13

Lay It Right Down

Not afraid to be me anymore.
Who cares what they think
since I like what I finally see!
Stood up for myself, and beauty
arrived to say hello. Sunshine
is the only happy feature
playing in my life.

This is my time to resurrect
the song that belongs inside
my heart. Celebrate the
masterpiece of original
design. Souls were born to
be free from the burden—
lay it right down. Give
patience of day, and show
me some tenderness.

Love me the way I am
with all my strength poured
out towards the finish line.
History will not repeat its
listing. My eyes touch the
unseen hope when I'm holding
Your hand. Stand and walk by
faith to live again.

Battleground

The deepest hurt cannot be expressed
    by mere words but by the way I must
follow to find the darkest hour of my soul.
    The water seems over my head right
now, and I'm too far from shore to reach
    land. I fear I shall be swallowed in this
great plan called life, with no purpose
    or disclosure.

I stand before You, having fought many
    battles, and yet I move on once again,
determined to learn who I am and
    resurrect the truth no matter the cost
displaced. Struggle is all I know, for now
    is the time to seek a quiet space to renew
my weary mind.

Mercy

When I feel like I just
can't go on, Yours is the
voice of reason that wills
me live, pouring out my
heart where only You can
hear my cries.

Let me see light—if only for
a little while—for it is in
Your care I taste it and
declare that goodness is
somewhere to be found.

Break not the bond that
clasps tight the pieces of
my life in turning Your
face from the broken way
that haunts my mind in
endless hours of wanting
mercy to appear as if hoping
for a miracle.

New Glasses

Change is so hard, like a
    calcium deposit in your
bathtub that just won't
    scrub off like bark until
you finally see green grass
    on the opposite side of black.

New glasses hanging around
    my head—just need to put them
on clearly. I begin to accept my
    new surroundings as high heels
wrapped around my ankles
    gently slip into view.

I like this newfound direction
    my feet take me in places. My
heart longs to stay comfortable
    in whom I am.

I Am More

I am more than just some autopilot nation. My words stand heroic to help others in need who cannot speak for themselves. Courage is found in the everyday living amongst rubble, believing the best.

Sunshine comes in various forms, but my favorite place is in a child smiling back at me, teaching me humility and grace.

Life has a way of passing by quickly, so don't let it drift away to the immersed. Grab ahold of the goodness and release your joy.

Revolution

I am the new revolution where being
normal is some term used by those
who only think they see right.

The wait is over, so let me run free,
for this is child's play at last—
I never got the chance.

Stand my ground—these limitless
possibilities. I wake, needing
authentic room to breathe.

Making Changes

Let the sun finally shine on this
    black screen called life. Swallow up
the madness seen with childlike
    eyes piercing hope into eternity,
forever fixed on a new way home.

Pieces of my heart are recognizable
    only by the connection of those willing
to alter time to listen to a barking
    conscience waiting to be heard in
momentary measure.

Making changes is what I must do to
    be free by any certain empowered
distance in the future, no matter what
    the cost or fear displaces, only to become
someone I love.

Standing Firm

Not alone in the silence of my
being as I breathe in this newfound
truth seared mindfully within
the knowledge that I am
a survivor.

I will not lose myself on the way
to find a joyful path, as I express my
right to become my own best friend,
remembering this inspiring role I
was given in God's great plan.

Standing firm with confidence,
I relentlessly fight for my life as if
to say I will gather those around who
love me to draw strength from above,
for I am beginning to see the honest sun.

Like a Cat with Nine Lives

You have no right to steal my joy,
no matter the stakes be high, for
my power is always of a greater
prudence.

Say what you will with utter disdain,
but my will conquers all the evident
lack of self-confidence you display
while destroying my honor.

I land on my feet like a cat with
nine lives, proceeding to tell
the truth of the matter at hand,
staying the victor with my head
held high.

Wounds in All of Us

There is a place deep within, where
we choke back the tears that lead
the trail of carefully buried wounds
in all of us.

Must we lay bare our true feelings
to get to the heart of the equation
causing an eruption of raw matter
we would rather forget?

Only truth will catapult us into a
new era of hard work to reveal the
healing inside this newfound
metamorphosis.

Unfamiliar Places

Forgiveness comes in unfamiliar
    places, trying to claim it for my
own, but so elusive like a shadow
    in the night.

A doorway partially left ajar by
    mistake—a risk I am willing to
sacrifice for the sake of learning
    how to love the woman looking back
at her self-reflection.

No more shame or guilt beguile,
    ruminating rampant in my head.
Sticking to the truth this time. No
    off-course rhythm playing mind
games that leave me with regret.

Awakening

Like a freight train jumping off
    the tracks for the hundredth time,
lack of breath headed straight
    toward my body with no time
to squeeze the trigger that came
    looking for the target running
down streams of unmeasurable pain.

This time she's likely to find the
    woman whose long-awaited
fighting spirit stands within her shattered
    ground unearthing all pride, finally
finding its way to some peace and
    happiness pouring a double portion,
as she barely begins to touch the
    awakening sky.

This Road I've Walked

This road I've walked, riddled with
pain, has been revealed as just a
sideline for the comfort I now share.

Hope is not lost in the tempest, yet
centered in the stillness of time that
sometimes progresses so slowly.

Stronger I grow, taking root, thirsty
for living this beautiful life, anxious
to see beyond what I can imagine.

Courage

It took courage to come out of the fire and live on my own terms, not afraid to open my eyes and accept the truth that once served as a reminder to enslave me in the past tense.

No more do I look upon the high price exacted with disdain, but with dignity, knowing I am a stronger person, fighting for my right to be heard like a lost soul that sings even when darkness surrounds.

While Looking

Mosaic pieces on the ground,
    broken are all I see. What
a beautiful picture they
    reveal if looking through
the obvious kaleidoscope!

Fly

Run with eagles for
they have vision to
impart wisdom on a
called journey, placed
in front of an otherwise
locked door.

Fly to your calling
as you seek the
master skill in your
hands to prepare the
art unearthly bound
in a fury of abandoned
thought.

The Power to Transform

I look inside, and it just keeps pouring
grit mixed with intense pressure, allowing
no surrender, looking forward to some
sweet breaking news.

Love life; rejoice in the small—revealed
through the belief of one's power to
transform.

Light the fire once beckoned, tearing
fear aside to let self prevail, breaking
the cusp of salvation.

Fierce

The essence of my destiny gives
    way to known fears finally put to
the test, as I embrace what I was
    born to capture in words set to
motion so fierce this world has
    not yet heard!

So, I move forward in confidence,
    realizing the past has forged my
spirit for a reason that I cannot
    fully appreciate, yet with eyes
half open, sleepily in gaze,
    wandering as best I can to the
music inside my head that creates
    a window inside my restored soul.

The Bravery of Power

A fire burning in my soul reminds
me of the power I capture,
like a photograph in this
gallery called life.

Becoming brave, peeling back expectations,
I find the strength to
preserve obstacles, knocking down
the hard places.

No more excuses; dreams are not
made of fear or procrastination.
So, choose a different path named
truth, believing in myself and
passionate visions that lead to
my destiny.

Warrior

Conviction cost everything in my mind
to believe, knowing I am worthy of all
God has in His divine riches stored just
for me.

I must lay hold of this strong faith I have;
grab with all my might, not for the faint
at heart, but one of a warrior.

Overflow with wisdom, pour out spoken
promises over my life as You prepare me
for my destiny. Fully trusting You have
gone before—step on over into the blessing;
tears have turned to joy!

The Struggle

My inner child desires
   to always give You highest honor,
seeking only to treasure and love You.

But, somehow, an irritable mouth opens
   and spews out words unbecoming
of the vessel worn out from
   the struggle of trying to understand
my role down a twisted path
   not of my own making.

Choke back the mistakes
   I have made. A change needs
to appear for me to survive
   this metamorphosis as I grow
older, looking to the future
   for a clean slate.

The Secret Key

I never grow tired
of learning how to love
you in this constant struggle
of independent wills.

Barriers that stood in our way
are in danger of crashing down
when compromise comes walking
in one another's shoes.

Listening is the anecdote
for this thirsty ground so needed
between us, like the secret key
that unlocks the passion
I so freely give.

The Open Door

Caged like an animal,
designed to live outside the
unknown boundaries, wrapped
inside this relentless prison
that haunts me.

Thinking about another direction,
my heart desires to explore
the discovery of an open door,
not stuck on the same
side of the mirror,
free to see the entire canvas.

The Meaning of Love

Love means sometimes you
let go of the control
aching to grasp
at any moment's notice.

Love means sometimes
putting your own desires
aside to sacrifice
and give support behind
someone else's dreams
so they become a reality.

Love means holding on,
tied to a ship's bow,
when you find yourself
in the middle of a relentless,
forceful wind.

Turn Around

Why are there only excuses
for why this communication
between us is nonexistent?

Two tin cans work
better than what we have,
tied up with all the hurt.
I am exposed and drained,
feeling like I'm giving more than
getting: one-sided.

Something must change the unhealthy
path; we seem to be headed
down a gridlock. Turn around
to see love encapsuled in
the solution working as one.

Waking Up

So tired of settling for
what I know. I deserve
more when inhabiting life
with a passion that cannot
be contained within walls of normalcy.

Experience, just waking up, is only
invited to the dance
inside my dreams.
Light the fire that burns bright,
so hear me now as
I begin to hunger.

My Life Rising

No matter what mere mortals may say,
there is a hope rising like
the water's edge, giving faith to an
otherwise painful situation.

My life will not be identified by others
who ransomed me, but by living like a
shooting star rising above in the midst
of a hurricane.

I shall conquer even these messy,
gut-wrenching days. Life shall not
swallow me!

Morsel of Faith

When you lose all sight of faith
    in the dregs and mire of what seems
to be the bottom of quicksand,
    there is a mysterious hand reaching
down to pull you up over the saving
    edge of reason.

Doubt creeps in, even though
    sentiments of hope want to wander,
like a stray cat looking for any morsel
    for which to feed itself.

Finding my way to the true me is a
    search for a rare treasure, one filled with
many meaningful adventures beyond
    a lesson all unto its own.

Back from the Abyss

Today was the end of all
that entwined us, hearing
nothing but silence like the
grave.

Your words pierce straight
to my heart, arrows flying,
pointing their aim towards
no other.

Never shall I return, for this
abyss has taken its toll, feeling
transported once more down
a road I walked before.

Moving forward with each
mechanical step, I vow to love
myself, giving perseverance
her name.

Before Midnight

My mind runs deep in oceans drifting,
    as if reaching for its returning ways.

This mysterious pattern, like the
    color of my jeans, burns ever
before midnight.

Stories help me tell where I've
    been in this grateful journey
I so lovingly weave.

The Other Given Half
A Perspective on Bipolar Disorder

In the middle of my mind sits
a necklace tangled so tightly,
seeking to stop the madness
caught by sheer anxiety.

Realizing the fears within drive
suspicions backwards, I fall
and offer my own name, black
pools of water escaping the
night that precedes my soul.

Sing now, for there is hope
after the dark rain, hurting no
more, only the sun appealing on
my behalf to make right the
other given half.

Sunshine

I am strong each moment in
the power of my thoughts,
sharing this journey that unfolds
before me.

Boldly, I step into the sunshine
of truth growing sweet like
wildflower honey on a Saturday
morning.

Light flows where beauty gives
peace, so easily bestowed in a
world needing grace.

Lemons for Breakfast

There are days I don't even
recognize myself when
irritability sets in like a
hot summer's day, lingering
over the horizon, dripping wet.

I hate what it makes me
become, like a disguise covering
my real face. Eating lemons
for breakfast is my mainstay.

Give me time out to reflect on
peace of mind, gaining strength
to forgive myself, beginning
again tomorrow.

Stronger

Stronger than credit is due, I
am a survivor of many strong
stones hurled by brokenness
misplaced.

Caring hearts take heed—giving
away your soul is not love's aim.

Yet, a lifetime of learning to be
one's true self leaves reborn
confidence only realized.

This grateful journey just
beginning has new eyes for
the path, which I now climb
within the blessings bestowed.

Remembering Intuitions

Saving myself from the mask
I wear is a tribute to discovering
the true face behind trying to
save the world.

Letting go to gain life in the
purest form, like seeing the
beauty in existence.

Don't have to try to impress
those lacking reciprocity.
Shut the door for a final
curtain call to those who gave
no boundaries.

Creating a safe space with
which to fill my soul, growing
in perfect place, learning to
hear intuitions speaking truth.

Called to Live Beauty

When life can't find the good in
circumstances rendered arduous,
I remember that hope never expires.
Lift my head in defiance of negativity
seeping in the cracks.

Wasting time with secrets bound by
silence that breaks the soul. Restitution
in forgiveness comes by way of faith
and love outpoured.

Bowing head, granting the given
wisdom to recall those who have
gone before. Stand to see the good
believed in me. Called to live beauty
in surrendered poise, fighting for grace
to take a front seat.

Praise for the rugged path that brought
back the light. Trusting Your mercy alone
covers my head and moves to silence the
darkness. Storms come to remind the present
healing sought to uplift the strength of character.

ABOUT THE AUTHOR

Martha Craig is a poet who lives in the heart of the Midwest. Her book *Driftwood* is a remarkable, honest portrayal of her life, showing the truth and beauty revealed in this body of art. Craig's journey of living with bipolar disorder and Post Traumatic Stress Disorder has led her to relate on a level with many different people and adapt in stressful situations, leaving her with a deep sense of honor for the lives of those who are hurting. She delivers a powerful, yet poignant, message that you are never alone.

Martha Craig believes it is her new-found, creative outlet and deep-abiding faith that have been her salvation. Her wish is that you see a way out of the darkness through her words. She sees that a challenge can be a gift to catapult you into a new perspective and give you strength you never knew. *Driftwood* is a unique collection of her poetry that pertains to all who feel a sense of loss and longing for hope to arrive.

Sign up for the TABLELAND PRESS newsletter

and receive this FREE ebook!

Beauty Takes a Breath is a five-poem introduction to Martha Craig's introspective style and optimistic voice that will refresh your mind. This exciting sample of her poetry is reflective of her words woven in opportunities of wisdom.

Each month you will receive a new poem from Martha Craig, as well as devotionals, Christian book reviews, Bible quizzes, and the latest news about upcoming books.

Download your free PDF of
Beauty Takes a Breath
at www.tablelandpress.com.

www.ingramcontent.com/pod-product-compliance
Lightning Source LLC
Chambersburg PA
CBHW061759070526
44586CB00023B/2631